Level 1	Part

MW00805970

STUDENT ACTIVITIES MANUAL
作业簿
for

Chinese Link

中　文　天　地

Zhōng　Wén　Tiān　Dì

Beginning Chinese

Second Edition

Simplified Character Version

吴素美　　于月明　　张燕辉　　田维忠

Sue-mei Wu　　Yueming Yu　　Yanhui Zhang　　Weizhong Tian

Pearson

Harlow, England • London • New York • Boston • San Francisco • Toronto • Sydney • Dubai • Singapore • Hong Kong
Tokyo • Seoul • Taipei • New Delhi • Cape Town • São Paulo • Mexico City • Madrid • Amsterdam • Munich • Paris • Milan

Senior Acquisitions Editor: Rachel McCoy
Editorial Assistant: Noha Amer
Publishing Coordinator: Kathryn Corasaniti
Executive Marketing Manager: Kris Ellis-Levy
Senior Marketing Manager: Denise Miller
Marketing Coordinator: William J. Bliss
Senior Media Editor: Samantha Alducin
Development Editor for Assessment: Melissa Marolla Brown
Media Editor: Meriel Martinez
Senior Managing Editor: Mary Rottino
Associate Managing Editor: Janice Stangel
Senior Production Project Manager: Manuel Echevarria
Senior Manufacturing and Operations Manager, Arts and Sciences: Nick Sklitsis
Operations Specialist: Cathleen Petersen
Senior Art Director: Pat Smythe
Art Director: Miguel Ortiz
Cover Image: Jochen Helle
Full-Service Project Management: Margaret Chan, Graphicraft Limited
Printer/Binder: Bind-Rite Graphics
Cover Printer: Demand Production Center
Publisher: Phil Miller

Copyright © 2011, 2006 Pearson Education, Inc., publishing as Prentice Hall, 1 Lake St., Upper Saddle River, NJ 07458. All rights reserved. Manufactured in the United States of America. This publication is protected by Copyright, and permission should be obtained from the publisher prior to any prohibited reproduction, storage in a retrieval system, or transmission in any form or by any means, electronic, mechanical, photocopying, recording, or likewise. To obtain permission(s) to use material from this work, please submit a written request to Pearson Education, Inc., Permissions Department, 1 Lake St., Upper Saddle River, NJ 07458.

This book was set in 12/15 Sabon by Graphicraft Ltd., Hong Kong.

Printed in the United States of America
23 2022

ISBN 10: 0-205-69638-4
ISBN 13: 978-0-205-69638-3

目录　CONTENTS

前言 PREFACE

The second edition of the *Student Activities Manual* for the *Chinese Link* contains homework assignments for each lesson in the main textbook. Homework activities are divided among listening exercises, character exercises, grammar exercises, and comprehensive exercises.

Thanks to the many instructors and students who provided valuable feedback on the first edition, the second edition incorporates several new features that we believe will make the materials more effective and easier to use. These new features are highlighted below:

1. For more efficiency and convenience, the *Workbook* is now divided into two separate volumes, the *Student Activities Manual* and *Character Book*.

   The new edition of the *Student Activities Manual* now provides a greater variety of exercises to consolidate what students have learned for each lesson. It incorporates listening, character, grammar and comprehensive exercises into each lesson's homework.

   The *Character Book* now combines both the traditional and simplified character versions.

2. More **challenging and authentic materials** have been added to the listening exercises. Situational dialogues have been created for each lesson that incorporate its themes, expressions, and its pragmatic settings of the lesson. Dialogues also contain some vocabulary and expressions that the students have not yet studied in the hope that these situational dialogues can challenge them from the very beginning and help them develop the skill of picking out useful information even if they don't fully understand everything they hear. This helps develop an important survival skill for students who will encounter real-life settings in Chinese society through study abroad, travel, or interaction with Chinese communities in their own countries.

3. At the end of each lesson's exercises, a **Progress Checklist** is included so that instructors and students can check that the students have accomplished the goals of the lesson and acquired the competencies that the lesson was designed to help them learn.

Sue-mei Wu 吳素美, Ph.D.
Lead author of *Chinese Link*
Carnegie Mellon University

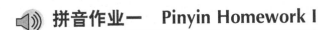

拼音作业一　Pinyin Homework I

Simple finals: a o e i u ü　　　*Labial initials: b p m f*　　　*Alveolar initials: d t n l*

1-1 Listen and choose the syllable you hear.

1. lū　lú　lǔ　lù　　　5. dē　dé　dě　dè
2. fū　fú　fǔ　fù　　　6. mō　mó　mǒ　mò
3. pī　pí　pǐ　pì　　　7. tī　tí　tǐ　tì
4. nā　ná　nǎ　nà　　　8. bā　bá　bǎ　bà

1-2 Listen and choose the syllable you hear.

1. mù　nù　　　4. lǔ　nǔ　　　7. lǔ　nǔ　　　10. nǐ　lǐ
2. pā　tā　　　5. pà　bà　　　8. bè　tè　　　11. tā　lā
3. mó　fó　　　6. tè　lè　　　9. dí　tí　　　12. pū　fū

1-3 Listen and write the Pinyin for the syllables you hear.

1. _____　　5. _____　　9. _____

2. _____　　6. _____　　10. _____

3. _____　　7. _____　　11. _____

4. _____　　8. _____　　12. _____

拼音作业二　Pinyin Homework II

Velar initials: g k h　　　　　*Palatal initials: j q x*
Dental sibilant initials: z c s　　*Retroflex initials: zh ch sh r*

2-1 Listen and choose the syllable you hear.

1. qì　xì	5. cè　chè	9. zhà　chà
2. xī　sī	6. zhè　zè	10. zǔ　shǔ
3. shī　sī	7. jī　qī	11. cǐ　sǐ
4. jǐ　xǐ	8. rì　shì	12. shú　chú

2-2 Listen and fill in the blanks with the initial sounds you hear.

1. ____ē	6. ____í	11. ____à
2. ____ī	7. ____ù	12. ____ú
3. ____è	8. ____ì	13. ____ǐ
4. ____ī	9. ____ū	14. ____è
5. ____ā	10. ____ē	15. ____ì

拼音作业三　Pinyin Homework III

Compound finals: ai ei ao ou　ia iao ie iu　ua uo uai ui　üe

3-1 Listen and mark the tones you hear.

1. lao	5. ren	9. lüe
2. cui	6. hou	10. shuai
3. zhua	7. hua	11. kuo
4. liu	8. ai	12. pei

3-2 Listen and choose the syllables you hear.

1. chóu　zhóu	6. cáo　cái	11. jiǎo　xiǎo
2. chāo　qiāo	7. lái　léi	12. miè　mèi
3. dōu　duō	8. lín　liú	13. lüè　nüè
4. jué　xué	9. dāo　dōu	14. xuē　xiē
5. huó　hóu	10. diū　duī	15. rào　ròu

3-3 Listen and fill in the blanks with the final sounds you hear.

1. b_____	6. t_____	11. h_____
2. p_____	7. n_____	12. j_____
3. m_____	8. l_____	13. q_____
4. f_____	9. g_____	14. x_____
5. d_____	10. k_____	15. zh_____

Nasal finals:　an en　　　ian in　　　uan un
　　　　　　　　ang eng ong　iang ing iong　uang

4-1 Listen and mark the tones you hear.

1. jiong
2. xian
3. hun
4. an
5. qin

6. lun
7. rong
8. fen
9. cang
10. mian

11. hen
12. qiang
13. heng
14. liang
15. ling

4-2 Listen and choose the syllables you hear.

1. juān　　jūn
2. zhèn　　shèn
3. qiáng　qióng
4. xiàng　xuàn
5. rǎn　　zhǎn

6. lín　　líng
7. tūn　　tuān
8. rēng　zhēng
9. kàn　　kèn
10. qǐng　xǐng

11. xióng　qióng
12. zhàn　　zhèn
13. háng　　huáng
14. huán　　huáng
15. jūn　　qūn

4-3 Listen and fill in the blanks with the final sounds you hear.

1. b_____
2. p_____
3. m_____
4. f_____
5. d_____

6. t_____
7. n_____
8. l_____
9. g_____
10. k_____

11. h_____
12. j_____
13. q_____
14. x_____
15. zh_____

拼音作业五 Pinyin Homework V

Special Pinyin and tonal rules

5-1 Listen and fill in the blanks with the Pinyin for the words you hear.

1. _____   6. _____   11. _____

2. _____   7. _____   12. _____

3. _____   8. _____   13. _____

4. _____   9. _____   14. _____

5. _____   10. _____   15. _____

5-2 Listen and mark the tones you hear for each "yi" (一) and "bu" (不) below. Be sure to remember the "yi-bu" tonal rules.

1. ____wǔ____shí
   一五一十

2. ____xīn____yì
   一心一意

3. ____zhāo____xī
   一朝一夕

4. ____chàng____hè
   一唱一和

5. ____mó____yàng
   一模一样

6. ____wén____wèn
   不闻不问

7. ____míng____bái
   不明不白

8. ____zhé____kòu
   不折不扣

9. ____sān____sì
   不三不四

10. ____bēi____kàng
    不卑不亢

11. ____sī____gǒu
    一丝不苟

12. ____chéng____biàn
    一成不变

13. ____wén____zhí
    一文不值

14. ____qiào____tōng
    一窍不通

15. ____chén____rǎn
    一尘不染

Comprehensive Pinyin Review

6-1 Listen and choose the words you hear.

1. dàng　dèng
2. lǔ　nǚ
3. wō　ōu
4. jié　zéi
5. jūn　zhēn

6. lǔ　liǔ
7. bīn　bīng
8. niè　lèi
9. dōu　tōu
10. zuō　cuō

11. yǔ　yǒu
12. lián　liáng
13. xiōng　jiōng
14. kǒu　gǒu
15. xià　xiào

6-2 Listen and write the Pinyin for the classroom expressions you hear.

1. _____

2. _____

3. _____

4. _____

5. _____

6. _____

Lesson 1   Greetings
第一课 问候

I. Listening Exercises

1-1   Listen to the dialogue between Mary and John. Then choose whether the following statements are true or false.

1. Mary 是学生。   True   False

2. John 也是学生。   True   False

3. Mary 是老师。   True   False

4. John 是老师。   True   False

1-2   Listen to the dialogue again and write it in Pinyin.

Mary: _____

John: _____

Mary: _____

John: _____

1-3   Listen to the challenge dialogue. Though there may be some words and phrases that are unfamiliar to you, see if you can understand the general meaning by using what you have learned. Then choose whether the following statements are true or false.

1. They greet each other.   True   False

2. They are both students.   True   False

1-4   Listen to the challenge dialogue again and choose the best answer for each of the following questions.

1. Which statement best describes the speakers?

   a. Both of them are teachers.

   b. One is a student, and the other is a teacher.

   c. One is a student and the other one is a teacher as well as a student.

II. Character Exercises

1-5 Match each Pinyin sentence with its Chinese characters.

_____ 1. Tā yě bú shì xuésheng. a. 你也是学生吗？

_____ 2. Wǒ shì xuésheng. Nǐ ne? b. 他是老师吗？

_____ 3. Nǐ yě shì xuésheng ma? c. 我是学生。你呢？

_____ 4. Wǒ bú shì lǎoshī. d. 他也不是学生。

_____ 5. Tā shì lǎoshī ma? e. 我不是老师。

1-6 Write the Chinese characters for the following words.

1. he _____   4. I _____   7. not _____

2. good _____   5. also _____   8. you _____

3. teacher _____ 6. student _____

III. Grammar Exercises

1-7 Complete the following sentences using the clues given in parentheses.

1. 你 _____ 。(a greeting)

2. 我 _____ 。(is a student)

3. 你 _____ 学生吗？ (is also)

4. 他也 _____ 老师。(is not)

5. 你 _____ ? ("and you?") 你 _____ 老师吗？ (also is not)

1-8 Match each question with the response that best answers the question.

_____ 1. 你是学生吗？ a. 他不是老师。

_____ 2. 我学中文，你呢？ b. 我也不是老师。

_____ 3. 他是老师吗？ c. 我是学生。

_____ 4. 我不是老师，你呢？ d. 我也学中文。

1-9 Rewrite each of the following sentences. Include the words in parentheses.

1. 他学生。(是)

_____

2. 我是学生，你是学生? (也、吗)

_____

3. 他是老师，他学生。(不、是)

_____

IV. Comprehensive Exercises

1-10 Number the sentences of the following dialogue in the correct order.

_____ 1. A: 你好!

_____ 2. B: 我不是学生，你呢?

_____ 3. A: 你是学生吗?

_____ 4. B: 他也是学生吗?

_____ 5. A: 不是，他是老师。

_____ 6. B: 你好!

_____ 7. A: 我是学生。

1-11 Using what you have learned in this lesson, complete the following dialogue.

A: 你好!

B: (1) _____!

A: 我是学生，(2) _____?

B: 我不是学生，(3) _____。

A: 他 (4) _____ 老师吗?

B: 是，(5) _____。

Progress Checklist

After this lesson, you should be able to use Chinese to:

(   ) exchange simple greetings,

(   ) express whether you are a student or a teacher,

(   ) express whether someone is a student or a teacher,

(   ) ask whether someone is a student or a teacher.

Lesson 2 Names
第二课 名字

 I. Listening Exercises

2-1   Listen to the dialogue for each question. Then choose the best answer for each question.

1. What is the person's surname?

   a. Hú   b. Lú   c. Wú

2. Which of the following is true?

   a. Wenying is a teacher.

   b. Xiaomei's classmate is a teacher.

   c. Dazhong Li is Wenying's classmate.

3. Which of the following is true?

   a. Yu Ying's teacher is Xiaowen Wu.

   b. Yu Ying is a teacher.

   c. Yu Ying is the man's name.

2-2   Listen to the challenge dialogue. Though there may be some words and phrases that are unfamiliar to you, see if you can understand the general meaning by using what you have learned. Then choose whether the following statements are true or false.

1. They tell each other their names.   True   False

2. The male speaker's name is Wang Wen.   True   False

2-3   Listen to the challenge dialogue again and choose the best answer for each of the following questions.

1. What is May's Chinese name?

   a. Wang Wen   c. Xiaoying

   b. Meiying   d. Xiaomei

2. What is the Chinese teacher's surname?

   a. His surname is Li.   c. His surname is Wu.

   b. His surname is Wang.   d. His surname is Wen.

II. Character Exercises

2-4 Each of the following sets of characters has a common radical. Write the common radical on the line for each set.

1. 好　她　姓　＿＿＿＿

2. 吗　叫　呢　＿＿＿＿

3. 请　谁　　　＿＿＿＿

2-5 Match each simplified character with its traditional form.

＿＿＿ 1. 学　　a. 誰

＿＿＿ 2. 谁　　b. 師

＿＿＿ 3. 吗　　c. 問

＿＿＿ 4. 问　　d. 嗎

＿＿＿ 5. 师　　e. 學

2-6 Write the Chinese characters for the following sentences.

1. Qǐngwèn, nín shì Lǐ lǎoshī ma?

＿＿＿＿＿＿＿＿＿＿＿＿＿＿＿＿＿＿＿＿＿＿＿＿＿＿＿＿＿＿＿＿＿＿＿＿

2. Nǐde tóngxué jiào shénme míngzi?

＿＿＿＿＿＿＿＿＿＿＿＿＿＿＿＿＿＿＿＿＿＿＿＿＿＿＿＿＿＿＿＿＿＿＿＿

III. Grammar Exercises

2-7 Use the words in the box to write two positive statements, two negative statements, and two questions. You may use each word as many times as you need.

叫	您	姓	名字	中文	是	请问	我
老师	她	的	同学	不	什么	吗	

_____

_____

_____

_____

_____

2-8 Write questions for the following answers. The underlined words provide clues as to what your questions should focus on.

1. 我姓<u>吴</u> 。 _____?

2. <u>她</u>叫李小英 。 _____?

3. 他是<u>我的同学</u> 。 _____?

4. 我的中文名字是<u>于文汉</u> 。 _____?

IV. Comprehensive Exercises

2-9 Translate the following phrases into Chinese.

1. My teacher's name

_____

2. His classmates

_____

3. Wenzhong Li's student

_____

4. Your Chinese name

_____

5. Her student's Chinese name

_____

2-10 Complete the following dialogue.

A: 你好！请问，(1) _____？

B: 我 (2) ____ 李，(3) _____ 学文。你呢？

A: (4) ____ 叫吴小英。我 (5) ____ 学生。

B: 她是 (6) ____？她 (7) _____ 学生吗？

A: 不，她是 (8) _____ 。

B: 她是 (9) _____ 中文老师吗？

A: 不，(10) _____ 我的英文老师 。

Progress Checklist

After this lesson, you should be able to use Chinese to:

(   ) ask someone's name politely,

(   ) tell others your name,

(   ) find out someone's name.

Lesson 3　Nationalities and Languages
第三课　国籍和语言

 I.　Listening Exercises

3-1　Listen to the short passage and then choose the best answer for each of the following questions.

1. What is Li Wenying's nationality?
   a. Chinese
   b. American
   c. Korean

2. What languages can Li Wenying speak?
   a. She can speak English, Chinese and Japanese.
   b. She can speak English, some French and Chinese.
   c. She can speak both Chinese and Japanese.

3. Who is Li Wenying's teacher?
   a. Fang laoshi
   b. Li laoshi
   c. Wang laoshi

4. Where is her teacher from?
   a. He is from China.
   b. He is from Japan.
   c. He is from Korea.

5. What languages can her teacher speak?
   a. He can speak English and a little French.
   b. He can only speak English and Chinese.
   c. He cannot speak French.

3-2　Listen to the challenge dialogue. Though there may be some words and phrases that are unfamiliar to you, see if you can understand the general meaning by using what you have learned. Then choose whether the following statements are true or false.

1. Guoying is Korean.	True	False
2. Guoying is Japanese.	True	False
3. Guoying can speak Korean.	True	False

3-3   Listen to the challenge dialogue again and choose the best answer for each of the following questions.

1. What languages can Guoying speak?

   a. He can speak Korean but not Japanese.

   b. He can speak Japanese but not Korean.

   c. He can speak both Korean and Japanese.

2. What is Guoying's nationality?

   a. He is Korean.

   b. He is Japanese.

   c. He is Chinese.

   d. He is American.

II. Character Exercises

3-4   Look at the pictures and identify the nationality of each person.

1.

_____

3.

_____

2.

_____

4.

_____

3-5 Write as many characters as you can that use the following radicals.

1. 讠 _____

2. 女 _____

3. 口 _____

III. Grammar Exercises

3-6 Complete the following sentences, using the clues given in parentheses.

1. 你是哪国人？

   我是 _____。(英)

2. 我是 _____ 人。(中)

   我说 _____。

3. 他是 _____。

   他教* _____。(英)

4. 我会 _____。(英)

   我也会 _____。(法)

   *Note: 教 [jiāo]: to teach

3-7 Complete the following sentences.

1. 小文是 _____，他 _____ 中文。

2. 李小美 _____ 法国人，她 ____ 说英文，她说 _____。

3. 她 ____ 美国人，她说 _____，她 ____ 说 _____ 日文*。

   *Note: 日文 [Rìwén]: Japanese language

IV. Comprehensive Exercises

3-8 Use the information that you compiled in class as a reference to write an introduction about a classmate. Write as much as you can. (Use approximately 60 characters.)

_____

_____

_____

_____

_____

_____

_____

Progress Checklist

After this lesson, you should be able to use Chinese to:

(   ) ask others their nationality and what language(s) they can speak,

(   ) tell others your nationality and what language(s) you can speak,

(   ) talk about others' nationalities and the language(s) they can speak.

Lesson 4   Studies
第四课 学习

 I. Listening Exercises

4-1   Listen to the short passage and then choose the best answer for each of the following questions.

1. What does Meiying study?

    a. Engineering

    b. English literature

    c. Chinese language

2. What does Meiying say about her teacher?

    a. He is an American. He can speak some Chinese.

    b. He is from Britain. He can speak some Chinese.

    c. He is from China. He can speak English.

3. Does Meiying find studying literature very difficult?

    a. No, not difficult at all.

    b. Yes, but only a little.

    c. Yes, very difficult.

4. Where is Xiaowen from?

    a. She is from the U.S.

    b. She is from China.

    c. She is from Britain.

5. What books does Xiaowen have?

    a. Books on Chinese literature.

    b. Books on English literature.

    c. Books on English language.

4-2 Listen and complete the dialogues.

1. **A:** Zhè shì shénme?

   B: Zhè shì _____.

   A: Gōngchéng _____?

   B: _____.

2. **A:** _____ shéi?

   B: Nà shì _____.

   A: Tā _____ ma?

   B: Tā _____.

3. **A:** Nǐ xué _____?

   B: Wǒ xué _____.

   A: Zhōngwén _____?

   B: Bú _____, kěshì _____.

4-3 Listen to the challenge dialogue. Though there may be some words and phrases that are unfamiliar to you, see if you can understand the general meaning by using what you have learned. Then choose whether the following statements are true or false.

1. Xiaomei thinks the Lesson 3 test is difficult.   True   False

2. Wenzhong thinks the Chinese homework is not too much.   True   False

3. Xiaomei studies Engineering and she thinks it is very hard.   True   False

4-4 Listen to the challenge dialogue again and choose the best answer for each of the following questions.

1. What is Wenzhong's major?

    a. Chinese literature   b. English literature   c. Engineering

2. What does Wenzhong think about the Chinese test?

    a. He thinks it is difficult.

    b. He thinks it is very easy.

    c. He thinks it is easy but there is too much homework.

3. What statement below is NOT true about Xiaomei.

    a. Xiaomei's major is English literature.

    b. Xiaomei's major is Engineering.

    c. Xiaomei thinks the Lesson 3 test is not too difficult.

II. Character Exercises

4-5 Match each Pinyin phrase with its Chinese characters.

_____ 1. shénme shū   a. 你学什么

_____ 2. nǐ xué shénme   b. 功课很多

_____ 3. gōngchéng nán ma   c. 这本呢

_____ 4. gōngkè hěnduō   d. 工程难吗

_____ 5. zhè běn ne   e. 什么书

4-6 Write as many characters as you can that use the following radicals.

1. 人/亻 _____

2. 讠 _____

3. 工 _____

III. Grammar Exercises

4-7 Unscramble the following sentences by placing the characters in the correct order.

1. 文学 / 我 / 英国 / 学

   _____

2. 也 / 我们 / 功课 / 的 / 不少

   _____

3. 一 / 书 / 本 / 中文 / 这是

   _____

4. 工程 / 不 / 也 / 难 / 太

   _____

5. 文学 / 吗 / 英国 / 你 / 学

   _____

6. 是 / 本 / 书 / 什么 / 那 / 一

   _____

4-8 Write as many questions as you can for the following sentences.

Example: 这是中文书。
这是什么?
这是什么书?

1. 这是文中的一本工程书。

_____

_____

2. 工程课的功课很多。

_____

_____

3. 英国文学不太难。

_____

_____

4. 中文功课很多，也很难。

_____

_____

IV. Comprehensive Exercises

4-9 Translate the following sentences into Chinese.

1. He is my Chinese literature professor.

   _____

2. Is that an engineering book?

   _____

3. French literature is not very difficult, but there is a lot of homework.

   _____

4-10 Your school newspaper is conducting a survey about studying and life on campus. Write a paragraph for the newspaper survey. Include a brief introduction of yourself and your studies. (Use approximately 70 characters.)

_____

_____

_____

_____

_____

_____

Progress Checklist

After this lesson, you should be able to use Chinese to:

( ) ask and explain what something is,

( ) tell others what you study,

( ) ask someone what they study,

( ) talk about whether a course is difficult or not,

( ) talk about the amount and difficulty of homework in a course.

Lesson 5   Introductions
第五课 介绍

 I. Listening Exercises

5-1   Listen to the dialogue. Then choose whether the following statements are true or false.

1. Xiǎohóng de shìyǒu jiào Měiwén.	True	False
2. Měiwén hé Fāng Míng dōu shì Zhōngguórén.	True	False
3. Fāng Míng jièshào tāde péngyou Xiǎohóng.	True	False
4. Měiwén cháng gēn Xiǎohóng shuō Zhōngwén.	True	False
5. Xiǎohóng méiyǒu Měiguó shìyǒu.	True	False

5-2   Listen to the dialogue and write the Pinyin for the words you hear.

吴小英：大文，我来 (1) _____ 一下 。这 (2) _____ 我室友
王小红 。

李大文： (3) _____ 李大文 。你好!

王小红：你好! 你是学生 (4) _____ ?

李大文：是 。我 (5) _____ 工程 。你 (6) _____ ?

王小红：我学 (7) _____ 。我 (8) _____ 小英 (9) _____ 同学 。
我们 (10) _____ 学 (11) _____ 文学 。

5-3   Listen to the challenge dialogue. Though there may be some words and phrases that are unfamiliar to you, see if you can understand the general meaning by using what you have learned. Then choose whether the following statements are true or false.

1. Wang Hong is Xiaomei's roommate.	True	False
2. Wenzhong doesn't have roommates.	True	False
3. Wenzhong often speaks Chinese with Xiaoying.	True	False

5-4 Listen to the challenge dialogue again and choose the best answer for the following questions.

1. Who are Wenzhong's roommates?

   a. Wang Hong and Xiaomei.

   b. Dingming and Fang Xiaowen.

   c. Xiaoying and Fang Xiaowen.

2. What are Wang Hong and Xiaoying's nationalities?

   a. They are both Korean.

   b. Wang Hong is Chinese. Xiaoying is American.

   c. They are both Chinese.

3. What statement below is NOT true?

   a. Xiaomei has two Chinese roommates.

   b. Wenzhong has two Chinese roommates.

   c. Xiaomei is studying Chinese but Wenzhong is not.

II. Character Exercises

5-5 Choose the correct traditional form for each of the following characters.

1. 来   a. 書   b. 來   c. 幾

2. 绍   a. 給   b. 麼   c. 紹

3. 几   a. 幾   b. 兒   c. 個

4. 两   a. 這   b. 兩   c. 國

5. 个   a. 兒   b. 來   c. 個

6. 这   a. 對   b. 這   c. 會

5-6 Write the Chinese characters for the following phrases.

1. liǎngge péngyou _____

2. jǐge shìyǒu _____

3. jièshào yíxià _____

4. cháng shuō Zhōngwén _____

III. Grammar Exercises

5-7 Unscramble the following sentences by placing the characters in the correct order.

1. 没 / 我 / 室友 / 有

   _____

2. 也 / 我们 / 常 / 都 / 中文 / 说

   _____

3. 两 / 他们 / 有 / 中国 / 个 / 室友

   _____

4. 都 / 老师 / 也 / 说 / 学生 / 中文 / 和

   _____

5. 几 / 室友 / 有 / 你 / 个

   _____

6. 常 / 我 / 跟 / 说 / 英文 / 我室友

   _____

5-8   Complete the following paragraph.

方美文 (1) _____ 中文班*的学生。她 (2) _____ 一个室友，
(3) _____ 王文英。

王文英 (4) _____ 中国人。她 (5) _____ 一个男朋友，(6) _____
李中。

李中是美国 (7) _____，他 (8) _____ 学中文。他常 (9) _____ 文英说
中文。

他们 (10) _____ 是好朋友。

*Note: 班 [bān]: class

5-9   Read the paragraph above. Write as many questions about the information as you can.
(Try to write at least four questions.)

_____

_____

_____

_____

_____

_____

_____

IV. Comprehensive Exercises

5-10 Your friend Wú Xiǎowén has come over to your apartment. You introduce Wú Xiǎowén to your roommates Wáng Fāng and Lǐ Yǒng. Write your introductions as a dialogue. Try to include things you have learned in this lesson and in previous lessons in the dialogue.

_____

_____

_____

_____

_____

_____

_____

Progress Checklist

After this lesson, you should be able to use Chinese to:

( ) introduce your friends to others,

( ) make small talk when first meeting others,

( ) find out if someone has roommates or not,

( ) find out how many roommates someone has.

Name: _____ Date: _____

Lesson 6 Family
第六课 家

 I. Listening Exercises

6-1 Listen to five statements. Then choose whether the following statements are true or false.

1. Jiāmíng hé Yǒupéng dōushì cóng Táiwān lái de.   True   False

2. Yǒupéng de bàba bù máng.   True   False

3. Jiāmíng méiyǒu nánpéngyou, tā jiějie yǒu.   True   False

4. Yǒupéng de jiā búzài Niǔyuē, zài Bōshìdùn.   True   False

5. Jiāmíng de mèimei méiyǒu māo, yǒu liǎngzhī gǒu.   True   False

6-2 Listen to the passage and questions. Then write the answers in Pinyin.

1. _____

2. _____

3. _____

4. _____

5. _____

6-3 Listen to the challenge dialogue. Though there may be some words and phrases that are unfamiliar to you, see if you can understand the general meaning by using what you have learned. Then choose whether the following statements are true or false.

1. Jenny is Mike's girlfriend.   True   False

2. Jenny's brother is also a student here.   True   False

6-4 Listen to the challenge dialogue again and choose the best answer for each of the following questions.

1. Where does Jenny come from?

   a. China   b. Britain   c. U.S.   d. France

2. Jenny's brother and Mike are

   a. good friends   b. roommates   c. classmates

II. Character Exercises

6-5 Write as many characters as you can that use the following radicals.

1. 女 _____

2. 人/亻_____

3. 车 _____

6-6 Write the Chinese characters for the following sentences.

1. Wǒ jiā yǒu sìge rén. _____

2. Jiějie yǒu yíge nánpéngyou. _____

3. Bàba, māma dōu shì zài Měiguó gōngzuò de. _____

4. Wǒ yǒu liǎngzhī gǒu. _____

5. Wǒ hěn ài wǒde jiā. _____

III. Grammar Exercises

6-7 Write the correct measure words.

1. 一____车   3. 两____学生

2. 一____狗   4. 三____书

6-8 Read the following passage. Then use 是……的 to answer the questions below.

小美的家在纽约。小美学英国文学，她也会说一点儿中文，她是在中国学中文的。她家有四个人：爸爸、妈妈、姐姐和她。爸爸、妈妈都是从北京来的，他们都在纽约工作。爸爸有两辆车，都是日本车。姐姐的男朋友叫家文，他是从英国来的。

1. 小美是学什么的？

   _____

2. 小美的爸爸、妈妈都是从哪儿来的？

   _____

3. 小美是在哪儿学中文的？

   _____

4. 姐姐的男朋友是从哪儿来的？

   _____

IV. Comprehensive Exercises

6-9 Translate the following sentences into Chinese.

1. Both Xiaoying and her boyfriend are from China.

   _____

2. My roommate has an American car.

   _____

3. There are four people in my family. We all love our families.

   _____

6-10 You have been looking for a Chinese pen pal (笔友 [bǐyǒu]), so you are very happy to receive an email from 李书文, a student in China who is also looking for a 笔友. Write a message to 李书文 that includes an introduction of yourself and your family. Then write some questions about him and his family.

_____

_____

_____

_____

_____

Progress Checklist

After this lesson, you should be able to use Chinese to:

(   ) introduce yourself and your family,

(   ) find out how many family members are in someone's family,

(   ) find out someone's occupation,

(   ) ask and tell people about where someone lives and works,

(   ) find out if someone has a car or any pets.

Lesson 7 Addresses
第七课 地址

I. Listening Exercises

7-1 Listen to the dialogue. Then choose the best answer for each of the following questions.

1. 小美住在哪儿?
   a. 住在宿舍。
   b. 住在校外。
   c. 住在朋友家。
   d. 住在公寓*。

2. 小美的房间号码是多少?
   a. 二三五
   b. 五二三
   c. 九二三
   d. 二八五

3. 公寓*的电话号码是多少?
   a. 三三二 二六八七四六九
   b. 七七二 二二八四七六九
   c. 五三三 六八六二四九七
   d. 八八二 九二八四六七三

4. 小美有几个室友?
   a. 四个
   b. 两个
   c. 三个
   d. 一个

*Note: 公寓 [gōngyù]: apartment

7-2 Listen and complete the dialogue in Pinyin.

常小西：书文，你住在那个 (1) _____ 吗?

程书文：不，我住在 (2) _____，房间号码是 (3) _____。

常小西：你的 (4) _____ 有 (5) _____ 吗?

程书文：没有 (6) _____，可是我有 (7) _____。

常小西：号码是 (8) _____?

程书文：号码是 (9) _____。

7-3 Listen to the challenge dialogue. Though there may be some words and phrases that are unfamiliar to you, see if you can understand the general meaning by using what you have learned. Then choose whether the following statements are true or false.

1. His home's street address number is 154.   True   False

2. His phone number is 452-234-0065.   True   False

7-4 Listen to the challenge dialogue again and choose the best answer for each of the following questions.

1. What is the context of the dialogue?

   a. Someone introducing their friend in a coffee shop.

   b. Two students running into their teacher in a grocery store.

   c. Someone giving an address in a post office.

   d. A waitress taking an order in a restaurant.

2. Which country is mentioned in the conversation?

   a. U.S.   b. France   c. Canada   d. China

II. Character Exercises

7-5 Match each Pinyin phrase with its Chinese characters.

_____ 1. duōshǎo hào   a. 电话号码

_____ 2. diànhuà hàomǎ   b. 你住在哪儿

_____ 3. Nǐ zhùzài nǎr   c. 我住校外

_____ 4. méiyǒu shǒujī   d. 多少号

_____ 5. Wǒ zhù xiàowài   e. 没有手机

7-6 Write the traditional forms of the following words.

1. 哪儿 _____   3. 房间 _____   5. 手机 _____

2. 号码 _____   4. 电话 _____

III. Grammar Exercises

7-7 Unscramble the following sentences by placing the characters in the correct order.

1. 的 / 你 / 吗 / 房间 / 大

   _____

2. 也 / 我们 / 校外 / 都 / 住 / 在

   _____

3. 的 / 他们 / 有 / 没有 / 电话 / 宿舍

   _____

4. 都 / 老师 / 住 / 宿舍 / 学生 / 在 / 和

   _____

5. 电话 / 是 / 多少 / 你的 / 号码

   _____

6. 吗 / 手机 / 有 / 你

   _____

7-8 大王 and 小李 are classmates who are exchanging contact information. Complete their conversation.

大王：小李，你 (1) ＿＿ 在宿舍吗？

小李：对了＊，我 (2) ＿＿ 在学校的 (3) ＿＿＿＿＿。你 (4) ＿＿ 住在学校的宿舍吗？

大王：不，我住在校外，在 (5) ＿＿＿＿＿＿＿＿＿＿＿ 第五大街＊。
　　　　　　　　　　　　　　　　　(Number 89764)

小李：你的房间 (6) ＿＿＿＿ 吗？

大王：很大，(7) ＿＿ 很好。你住在 (8) ＿＿＿＿＿？

小李：二〇八号。我的房间 (9) ＿＿ 不小。你的电话号码
　　　(10) ＿＿＿＿＿？

大王：(11) ＿＿＿＿＿＿＿＿＿＿＿
　　　　　　　(103-952-8467)

小李：我的电话号码 (12) ＿＿＿＿ 六四八二五三一。

＊*Notes*: 对了 [duìle]: yes, correct; by the way
　　　　第五大街 [dì wǔ dàjiē]: Fifth Ave.

IV. Comprehensive Exercises

7-9 Translate the following sentences into Chinese.

1. Where do you live?

   _____

2. Do you live on campus?

   _____

3. My brother's dorm is not big.

   _____

4. Is your cell phone number (142) 268-5738?

   _____

7-10 One of your friends is going to visit you over the weekend. Write a short note to your friend, providing information such as your address, phone number, roommates' names, and anything else that you think they might need to know.

   _____

   _____

   _____

   _____

   _____

   _____

Progress Checklist

After this lesson, you should be able to use Chinese to:

(   ) tell others your address and phone/cell phone number,

(   ) ask someone's address and phone/cell phone number,

(   ) find out where someone lives,

(   ) ask details about others' dorm rooms (e.g. room number, big or small, etc.).

Lesson 8   Meeting and Making Plans
第八课 见面、相约

 I. Listening Exercises

8-1 Listen to the questions and read the following answers. Then choose the best answers for the questions.

1. a. 对。那是我的中文书。
   b. 不对，那是我的中文书。
   c. 对。那是我的英文书。

2. a. 是，我是从韩国来的。
   b. 不是，我是从法国来的。
   c. 不是，我是从韩国来的。

3. a. 我室友的功课很多。
   b. 很多。
   c. 我今天没有事儿。

4. a. 他不在家。
   b. 我的家很大。
   c. 他的家不大。

8-2 Listen to the dialogue. Then choose the best answer for each of the following questions.

1. 德朋是从哪儿来的?
   a. 中国   b. 韩国   c. 纽约   d. 日本

2. 文中、德朋和王红今天想去吃什么菜?
   a. 中国菜   b. 韩国菜   c. 泰国菜   d. 日本菜

3. 他们下次想去吃什么菜?
   a. 中国菜   b. 韩国菜   c. 泰国菜   d. 日本菜

8-3 Listen to the challenge dialogue. Though there may be some words and phrases that are unfamiliar to you, see if you can understand the general meaning by using what you have learned. Then choose whether the following statements are true or false.

1. They will invite another person to join them tonight.   True   False

2. They will meet at the restaurant.   True   False

8-4 Listen to the challenge dialogue again and choose the best answer for each of the following questions.

1. What are they talking about?

    a. Their teachers   c. Their homework

    b. Going out together   d. Their apartment

2. Who knows Zhang Yongjun?

    a. Both of them know him.

    b. One knows him, but the other doesn't know him yet.

    c. Neither of them knows him.

    d. Neither of them knows him but they are going to meet him soon.

II. Character Exercises

8-5 Write the traditional forms of the following characters.

1. 认 _____   3. 课 _____   5. 饭 _____

2. 识 _____   4. 后 _____   6. 样 _____

8-6 Write the Chinese characters for the following sentences.

1. Nǐ yǒu shénme shèr ma?

   _____

2. Nǐ xiǎngbuxiǎng huí jiā?

   _____

3. Wǒmen yìqǐ qù Zhōngguó, hǎobuhǎo?

   _____

4. Xiàkè yǐhòu wǒ xiǎng qù péngyou jiā.

   _____

5. Wǒ bú rènshi nà ge gōngchéngshī.

   _____

III. Grammar Exercises

8-7 Match each question with the response that best answers the question.

_____ 1. 你认识不认识他?   a. 我想吃韩国菜。

_____ 2. 你想不想吃韩国菜?   b. 我不认识他。

_____ 3. 我们下次吃日本菜，怎么样?   c. 我没有事儿。

_____ 4. 下课以后你有事儿吗?   d. 行,很好。

8-8 Change the following sentences into questions using the words or patterns in parentheses.

1. 吴小美是学工程的。(是吗)

   _____

2. 她今天想回家。(A 不 A)

   _____

3. 张友朋认识我姐姐。(对不对)

   _____

4. 他的两个室友都是美国人。(吗)

   _____

5. 我们下次一起去纽约。(怎么样)

   _____

6. 下课以后我去吃饭。(A 不 A)

   _____

IV. Comprehensive Exercises

8-9 Translate the following sentences into Chinese.

1. Where are you going?

   _____

2. I have plans after class.

   _____

3. Do you want to have dinner with us tonight?

   _____

4. My friend doesn't know our English teacher.

   _____

8-10 You are going to invite your Chinese friend 文英 to watch a movie (电影 [diànyǐng]) after class. Write a short dialogue between you and 文英. Be sure to use "A 不 A" questions and tag questions in your dialogue.

   _____

   _____

   _____

   _____

   _____

   _____

   _____

Progress Checklist

After this lesson, you should be able to use Chinese to:

( ) ask someone where they are going,

( ) ask someone if they are free to do something with you,

( ) find out if someone knows another person,

( ) discuss with others what kind of cuisine you would like to eat,

( ) make plans to go out to eat.

Lesson 9　Phone Calls
第九课　打电话

I. Listening Exercises

9-1　Listen to the dialogue. Then choose the best answer for each of the following questions.

1. 丁明在哪儿?
   a. 在纽约
   b. 在他的房间
   c. 在朋友家
   d. 在宿舍

2. 丁明在做什么?
   a. 在看电视
   b. 在上网
   c. 在上课
   d. 在吃日本菜

3. 今天晚上丁明想做什么?
   a. 想看电影
   b. 想去朋友家
   c. 想看中文书
   d. 想上网

4. 和丁明打电话的是谁?
   a. 爱文
   b. 小美
   c. 丁明的妹妹
   d. 王红

9-2　Listen to the passage. Then choose whether the following statements are true or false.

1. 电话是小西的同学打来的 。　　　　　True　　　　　False

2. 打电话的人今天晚上想和小西一起去吃饭 。　　True　　　　　False

3. 他的电话号码是(一四二)三六六七八九二。　　True　　　　　False

9-3   Listen to the challenge dialogue. Though there may be some words and phrases that are unfamiliar to you, see if you can understand the general meaning by using what you have learned. Then choose whether the following statements are true or false.

1. He called a wrong number.   True   False

2. He was looking for his brother.   True   False

9-4   Listen to the challenge dialogue again and choose the best answer for each of the following questions.

1. What is the relationship between the two people?

   a. teacher and student   b. friends   c. classmates   d. strangers

2. What is her phone number?

   a. 65617085   b. 65618074   c. 65714078   d. 65610784

II. Character Exercises

9-5   Choose the Pinyin that correctly shows the pronunciation of the following characters.

1. 正在	zèngzài	zhèngzài	zèngzhài
2. 房间	hángjiān	féngjiàn	fángjiān
3. 电视	diànsì	diànshì	diánshì
4. 上网	shángwǎng	shàngwǎng	shánghuǎng
5. 时候	shíhou	shéhou	chíhou
6. 今天	zīntiān	jíntian	jīntiān
7. 晚上	wǎngsàng	wánchàng	wǎnshang
8. 留言	lúyán	niúyán	liúyán
9. 再见	zàijiàn	zhàijiàn	zhuáizhuàn
10. 知道	jīdào	jīdòu	zhīdào

9-6 Write the common radical for each of the following sets of characters.

1. 今 做 位 候 _____

2. 叫 呢 吗 吃 _____

3. 忙 怎 想 _____

4. 字 学 _____

5. 家 宿 室 _____

9-7 Write the traditional forms of the following words and phrases.

1. 打电话 _____   5. 对不起 _____

2. 看电视 _____   6. 时候 _____

3. 上网 _____   7. 谢谢 _____

4. 看书 _____   8. 给 _____

III. Grammar Exercises

9-8 Complete the following dialogue using "正在……" and the phrases in parentheses.

A: 请问小文在吗？

B: 在，他 (1) _____ 。(看电视)

A: 丁老师呢？

B: 她 (2) _____ 。(休息)

A: 姐姐呢？

B: 她 (3) _____ 。(和男朋友打电话)

A: 王红和小美都在学中文吗？

B: 王红没有在学中文。她 (4) _____ 。(学法文)

9-9 Unscramble the following sentences by placing the characters in the correct order.

1. 正在 / 我 / 呢 / 室友 / 电视 / 看

   _____

2. 就是 / 请问 / 哪位 / 是 / 我 / 您

   _____

3. 不在 / 他们 / 都 / 他们 / 正在 / 上课

   _____

4. 什么 / 老师 / 回来 / 时候 / 请问

   _____

5. 上网 / 室友 / 没有 / 在 / 他

   _____

6. 回来 / 给 / 请他 / 打电话 / 以后 / 我

   _____

IV. Comprehensive Exercises

9-10 Translate the following sentences into Chinese.

1. Would you like to leave a message?

   _____

2. Please ask him to call me when he returns.

   _____

3. May I ask who is speaking, please?

   _____

4. He's not watching TV. He's surfing the Internet.

   _____

5. Hold on, please.

   _____

9-11 Tonight you would like to go to see your classmate from Chinese class and ask some questions about your homework. You call but your friend doesn't answer the phone so you leave a message on the voice mail. Write your message below, being sure to include your reason for calling and asking your friend to give you a call back when your friend returns.

   _____

   _____

   _____

   _____

   _____

Progress Checklist

After this lesson, you should be able to use Chinese to:

(　) make and answer phone calls,

(　) ask a caller to wait a moment,

(　) tell someone they have a phone call,

(　) let someone know they dialed the wrong number and apologize when you dial the wrong number,

(　) leave and take messages,

(　) ask what someone is doing at the moment,

(　) tell others what you are doing at the moment.

Lesson 10　Time and Schedules
第十课　时间表

🔊 **I.　Listening Exercises**

10-1　Listen to 小美's daily schedule for her summer Chinese course in Shanghai, and then choose whether the following statements are true or false.

1. 小美每天早上八点起床。	True	False
2. 然后九点去学校上课。	True	False
3. 下课以后，小美常去图书馆看书。	True	False
4. 下午小美上中文课。	True	False
5. 中文课以后，小美去吃饭。	True	False

10-2　Listen to 友朋 talk about his daily schedule and write the time of each activity in Chinese.

1. 起床　　　3. 去学校　　　5. 去图书馆　　　7. 上中文课

　　_____　　　_____　　　_____　　　_____

2. 睡觉　　　4. 吃晚饭　　　6. 打球　　　8. 上网

　　_____　　　_____　　　_____　　　_____

10-3　Listen to the challenge dialogue. Though there may be some words and phrases that are unfamiliar to you, see if you can understand the general meaning by using what you have learned. Then choose whether the following statements are true or false.

1. They will go to class together this morning.	True	False
2. They will go to the library together after class.	True	False

10-4　Listen to the challenge dialogue again and choose the best answer for the following questions.

1. What is the time now?

　　a. 8:30　　　b. 9:00　　　c. 9:15　　　d. 9:30

2. When will their class begin today?

　　a. 9:30　　　b. 10:30　　　c. 10:45　　　d. 11:15

II. Character Exercises

10-5 Match the Pinyin with the corresponding Chinese characters.

_____ 1. jǐdiǎn qǐchuáng   a. 写电子邮件

_____ 2. shí'èrdiǎn bàn shuìjiào   b. 九点一刻

_____ 3. xiě diànzǐ yóujiàn   c. 几月几号

_____ 4. jiǔdiǎn yí kè   d. 几点起床

_____ 5. jǐ yuè jǐ hào   e. 十二点半睡觉

10-6 Write the Chinese characters for the following words and phrases.

1. university _____   5. email _____

2. semester _____   6. library _____

3. every day _____   7. to like _____

4. life _____   8. to write a letter _____

III. Grammar Exercises

10-7 Match each Chinese sentence with its meaning.

_____ 1. 他昨天八点才吃晚饭。

a. He was very busy yesterday and got up at six o'clock.

_____ 2. 他常常晚上三点以后才睡觉。

b. He didn't eat dinner until eight o'clock yesterday.

_____ 3. 他今天很忙，两点才吃午饭。

c. He often doesn't go to bed until after three o'clock.

_____ 4. 他昨天很忙，六点就起床。

d. He is not busy. He often doesn't get up until eleven o'clock.

_____ 5. 他不忙，他常早上十一点才起床。

e. He is very busy today and didn't eat lunch until two o'clock.

10-8 Unscramble the following sentences by placing the characters in the correct order.

1. 十点 / 我 / 二十 / 下课 / 分

   _____

2. 打球 / 去 / 以后 / 下课 / 我 / 喜欢

   _____

3. 邮件 / 地址 / 电子 / 我的 / 这是

   _____

4. 我 / 室友 / 生活 / 这是 / 大学 / 的

   _____

5. 睡觉 / 起床 / 几点 / 每天 / 他 / 几点

   _____

IV. Comprehensive Exercises

10-9 Translate the following sentences into Chinese.

1. He went to have Japanese food at 12:30. After that, he went to the library.

   _____

2. After getting up, I wrote a letter to my older sister.

   _____

3. He plays ball at 9:00 P.M. every day.

   _____

4. I like my university life.

   _____

10-10 Write a letter to a friend describing your daily schedule. (Use approximately 60 characters.)

_____

_____

_____

_____

_____

_____

_____

Progress Checklist

After this lesson, you should be able to use Chinese to:

( ) ask and give times in Chinese,

( ) express days, months and years in Chinese,

( ) ask someone about their daily schedule and tell others about your daily schedule,

( ) make small talk with others about your daily activities, studies, family and friends,

( ) write letters or emails to your family and friends describing your daily activities.

Lesson 11   Ordering Food
第十一课 点菜

 I. Listening Exercises

11-1   Listen to the dialogue. Then choose whether the following statements are true or false.

1. 他们正在饭馆吃饭 。   True   False

2. 美英正在喝汤 。   True   False

3. 饭馆的炒面不太好吃 。   True   False

4. 美英不喜欢喝可乐 。   True   False

11-2   Listen to the telephone conversation between 方小文 and a waitress at a Chinese restaurant. Choose the cost of each item that 方小文 ordered for pick-up.

Note: 拿 [ná]: pick up

方小文点的菜：

水   1   2   3   4   5

可乐   1   2   3   4   5

冰红茶   1   2   3   4   5

汤   1   2   3   4   5

炒饭   1   2   3   4   5

炒面　　　1　　2　　3　　4　　5

饺子　　　10　　20　　30　　40　　50

11-3 Listen to the challenge dialogue. Though there may be some words and phrases that are unfamiliar to you, see if you can understand the general meaning by using what you have learned. Then choose whether the following statements are true or false.

1. They are talking about what are they going to cook tonight.　　True　　False

2. He ordered noodles and dumplings.　　True　　False

3. He also ordered some cola.　　True　　False

11-4 Listen to the challenge dialogue again and choose the best answer for the following questions.

1. What is the conversation about?
   a. Ordering food from a Chinese restaurant.
   b. Inviting friends to eat.
   c. Going to watch a movie.
   d. When classes will start.

2. How long will it take for the food to be ready?
   a. 10 minutes　　b. 15 minutes　　c. 20 minutes　　d. 25 minutes

II. Character Exercises

11-5 Choose the correct traditional form for each of the following characters.

1. 双　　a. 雙　　b. 歡　　c. 幾
2. 乐　　a. 後　　b. 車　　c. 樂
3. 面　　a. 這　　b. 麵　　c. 紹
4. 还　　a. 還　　b. 這　　c. 湯
5. 员　　a. 盤　　b. 見　　c. 員
6. 务　　a. 員　　b. 務　　c. 兒

11-6 Write the Chinese characters for the following words.

1. xǐhuān _____

2. háishì _____

3. xiānsheng _____

4. lǜchá _____

5. chǎomiàn _____

6. kělè _____

7. fànguǎn _____

8. xiǎojiě _____

9. fúwùyuán _____

10. jiǎozi _____

III. Grammar Exercises

11-7 Ask questions using 还是 and the choices given below. Then answer each question.

1. 吃中国菜，吃法国菜

_____?

_____

2. 去打球，去图书馆

_____?

_____

3. 两点下课，三点下课

_____?

_____

4. 是工程师，是老师

_____?

_____

5. 有四门课，有五门课

_____?

_____

11-8 Choose an appropriate measure word from the box to complete the following sentences. Note that some measure words may be used more than once.

位 只 个 杯 瓶 辆 盘 碗 双 本

1. 常先生是一＿＿ 很好的老师。

2. 我点两＿＿ 炒饭和两＿＿ 可乐。

3. 爸爸有一＿＿ 狗。

4. 我们家有四＿＿ 人。

5. 她想喝一＿＿ 茶。

6. 我的朋友要一＿＿ 水。

7. 那个美国人有一＿＿ 车。

8. 那三＿＿ 法国人想喝一＿＿ 冰红茶和两＿＿ 咖啡。

9. 这五＿＿ 学生有三＿＿ 工程书。

10. 给我们三＿＿ 汤和一＿＿ 筷子。

IV. Comprehensive Exercises

11-9 Translate the following sentences into Chinese.

1. Do you like to drink tea or coffee?

   _____

2. Which do you like to study, literature or engineering?

   _____

3. After eating fried rice, I often want to drink a cup of tea.

   _____

4. I often go to Chinese restaurants.

   _____

11-10 Some of your friends are coming to visit you at your apartment this evening. Since you are too busy to cook, you plan to order from a nearby Chinese restaurant. Leave a note and ask your roommate to do you a favor and order the food. Be sure to include the following words and phrases in the note, as well as other words and phrases you have learned. (Use at least 70 characters.)

点　要　想　喜欢　杯　瓶　盘　碗　双　谢谢

_____

_____

_____

_____

_____

_____

_____

_____

_____

Progress Checklist

After this lesson, you should be able to use Chinese to:

( ) order food and drinks in a Chinese restaurant,

( ) ask and answer questions that present choices,

( ) express amounts of food and drink using common measure words,

( ) talk about going out to eat.